BAD NEWS
PAUL BIRTILL

Paul Birtill was born in Walton, Liverpool in 1960, but now lives in London. He has published a number of collections with Hearing Eye, including *New and Selected Poems*. He is also an accomplished playwright and several of his plays have been staged at London theatres, including *Squalor*, which was short-listed for the prestigious Verity Bargate award.

Bad News
Paul Birtill

ISBN 978-1-9031107-3-7

First published in this edition 2020 by Wrecking Ball Press.

Cover design: humandesign.co.uk

LOTTERY FUNDED   Supported using public funding by
ARTS COUNCIL ENGLAND

ACKNOWLEDGEMENTS:

Some of these poems first appeared in Poetry Review,
The Spectator, Morning Star, G.O.B. and Rising.

CONTENT

BAD NEWS

I'm always hearing of people dying,
especially now I'm getting older.
Somebody is always telling me someone
I know has died. And soon, somebody
somewhere will be telling someone in
a casual way I have died. I can almost
hear it being said – 'Paul the poet's dead.'

COMPANION

The old woman invalid advertised
in the Lady magazine for a companion.
What she got was a paranoid schizophrenic.
She seemed quite normal at first, but then came
the laughter at night and banging of doors -
straight out of Jane Eyre. Then she noticed
her companion was taking more tablets than she was,
which set alarm bells ringing and when she asked her
to leave, was locked in her bedroom for three days
without food. Only a relative who came calling saved
her from imminent death. Her mad companion was nowhere
to be found. She had done a bunk with the hall clock.

OUTCOME

Not long before he died,
my dad told me that as a young man
he was often worried and anxious
about how his life would all turn out
and the seemingly endless years that lay ahead.
'Was it as you imagined?' I asked him.
'Not really' he said – 'it's been nothing short
of a bloody disaster.' Approaching old age
I could now say the same about mine, but at least
there are no children to repeat my mistakes –
carry on the depressing cycle – it ends with me.

THE PRACTICE

He mistook my number for some medical
practice in Harlow and kept leaving
annoying messages on my answer phone,
until finally I rang him back and said
I was calling from the practice and to
stop leaving us rude messages. 'I didn't
leave any rude messages' he said. 'I think
you're looking for a slap' I said. 'Who am
I talking to?' he asked sounding surprised.
'I'm the practice manager and you smell,
you smell the practice out every time you come in.'
'What the hell's going on' he shouted, 'I'm coming
down there' and slammed the phone down.

INVITATION TO DINNER

My rude friend invited me round
for a meal yesterday. 'What are
we having?' I asked. 'You'll take
what you're given and be glad of it'
he said. 'And don't come empty-handed,
bring something to the table — a good
bottle of wine — something we can all share.
After all, I'm making the dinner.' 'And what
are we having?' I enquired again. 'You'll
take what you're given' he said. 'And don't
take anything from the flat.'

CONVERT

My father became a Roman Catholic
without telling his parents in his late teens.
His mother, a parson's daughter, didn't approve
of Catholicism and my father used to hide
Catholic Truth Society literature under his pillow,
in the same way I used to hide nude magazines under
mine from him. He decided he wanted to be a priest
in 1940, but was told by the bishop in no uncertain
terms, there could be no vocations in wartime for young
men, so he married my mother.

CHOICES

I preferred drinking to womanising
as a young man. I was good-looking
and got lots of dates, but they never
really went anywhere. I would take them
on a pub-crawl and get quite drunk which
they always hated. Then at thirty-five I
got fat and all that was suddenly over.
It took some getting used to being fat and
unattractive to women and I regretted not
meeting my soul-mate when I had the chance,
and the rather lonely life that followed,
but at least I still had the drink and no one
to disturb me.

GUESS WHO'S COMING TO DINNER?

Schizophrenics often have delusions
and my sister became obsessed with
the newscaster Kenneth Kendall in the
eighties – sent him dozens of letters.
She received the standard signed photo
from the BBC. Then she told us he was
coming to visit us on the tenth of June
at 6pm. Me and my dad laughed, but on that day
she cleaned the house from top to bottom and
prepared a special meal. We thought she was crazy,
but looked a little nervously at each other when
the doorbell rang at 6pm. 'Surely not' my dad said,
but it was the pools man earlier than usual. My sister
looked sad and never mentioned him again.

A BIT OF A DISAPPOINTMENT

He wasn't very happy in heaven,
it took him a while to settle down
and accept he was dead. The eternity
angle bothered him too – he couldn't
imagine being there forever, even in
his altered state – never being able
to die suddenly seemed rather unattractive.
He missed his body as well and trying to identify
people was proving very difficult. God wasn't all
he'd been cracked up to be either. In fact he'd snubbed
him twice in the telly lounge. No, he missed life
on earth with all its uncertainties and insecurities
and the knowledge it would some day end.

THE WALKER

He was very mean with his money –
hated spending a penny, but loved walking,
especially because it was free. You'd invite him
out for a drink and he'd say let's go for a walk
instead it doesn't cost anything. So you'd go for a walk
with him and after an hour or two when you were really tired,
you'd suggest going for a drink, but he'd say no, let's walk
some more – save our cash. He had a girlfriend for a while
and on her twenty-first birthday she suggested going for a
meal, but he insisted they went for a walk and bring
sandwiches – it's better value for money, he said. No wonder
then she chucked him – told him to take a walk.

THE GAS FIRE

We had it installed in the living-room
in the winter of 1970. It had a number
of buttons and switches on it, including
one that my father said if you pressed it
the thing would blow up. For years I believed
this to be the case and was careful not to touch
the button that would cause an explosion.
But then a friend pointed out – why would they
put a button on it that would cause it to blow up
if you pressed it and I realised my dad had been
talking nonsense. So I pressed it and the thing blew up.

FALL OUT

I had to make up with him in the end,
he had begun shouting things at me
in the street, bellowing insults from across
the road – embarrassing. So we met down the local
pub again and I apologised for calling his Irish
father a traitor and an idiot for joining the British
Army. He was okay about it and shook my hand – said he
was sorry for spitting beer in my face, but the friendship
I felt was a little fractured, they often are after a big
argument, never quite the same. It can be difficult to get
back to where you were.

FAREWELL

When I went back to Liverpool that Easter,
I was in a sorry state and someone said
I reminded them of a whipped dog.
Certainly I'd been treated quite cruelly
by the woman I was hopelessly in love with
and it must have showed. But I was glad to
get back home – see old faces, walk down
familiar roads, spend some time with my father –
we went to mass together on Easter Sunday,
I felt I needed one. I didn't realise it would be
the last time I ever saw him, that Easter holiday.
We shook hands when I was leaving like we always did.

DUELLING

I think I would have chickened out
of a duel in the eighteenth century –
just not turned up, kept them waiting
with their pistols at dawn and I wouldn't
have minded the dishonour and being called
a coward and a blaggard. They could have called
me anything they liked, as long as I didn't get shot.
Yes, I would have made it a regular thing, calling
people out, getting the customary slap in and then
not turning up, until eventually someone would have shot me
while I was having lunch in the pub.

ENTRIES

Such fun we had playing in entries
as children – kicking bins over,
letting off fireworks, smoking.
You sometimes found interesting things
in them too and they always seemed to attract
stray dogs. They were also the place for after-school
fights, as well as handy short-cuts to other roads
and great places to hide. But then the council put metal
gates up and blocked them all off – to prevent crime
they said – but the area is not the same now. I miss them,
they were part of my growing up.

DEAD PRIESTS

I feel like waking them up –
the sad fools lying in their damp
coffins for hundreds of years and
asking them did it actually happen –
the glorious resurrection, as they preached
it would? Are they really in heaven with their
loving God? And were their religious devotions
justified? Are they truly in paradise or just
rotting corpses beneath the earth? But I can't ask
and they certainly can't answer, heaps of putrid bones
as they surely are.

TWENTY-FOUR

When my dad caught me smoking at eight,
he told me to promise him that I wouldn't
smoke again till I was twenty-four.
I don't know why twenty-four and it seemed
like a long wait for my next fag. Then when
I was ten he caught me drinking alcohol and
told me to promise him I wouldn't drink again
till I was twenty-four, and a few years later
when I was thirteen he caught me having a wank
and told me to promise him I wouldn't do it again
till I was twenty-four. But all this abstention
was too hard for me and I cracked one afternoon
when I was fifteen and had a smoke, a drink and
a wank in my bedroom. My dad walked in and was shocked.
'You shouldn't be doing any of this till you're twenty-four'
he shouted. 'Sorry dad I couldn't wait' I said.

SEX ON TV

Whenever a sex scene came on the television,
my Catholic father would immediately jump up
and turn the set off. Then he'd stand there
looking at his watch, until he thought a reasonable
period had passed and turn it back on again.
I remember this happening a lot in James Bond films.
I had problems with girls growing up.

INTROSPECTION
(AFTER ELIOT)

It is the catastrophe that they never mentioned
which destroys each idle thought and can be measured
by another's fate in an unused vacuum of fear.
Better then that we go into this darkness blindly
without a care for its minor and depressing detail,
but carry on the search for the unknown quantity
that it professes to understand and sympathise with –
yet can only touch upon its defeated images. There are
changes afoot that we are only partially aware of and
if we continue to vacillate might miss completely and
remain in doubt forever. We must then begin the unconscious
transfer of strong unacceptable emotions from one object
to another in order to reveal its true meaning and define
its purpose.

CHRISTMAS

I bought a large family turkey
for me and the cat this Christmas –
feeds six it said on the label,
but I ate the lot. On New Year's Eve
I was kept awake by a party next door,
which spilled out into the garden.
I shouted at them to keep the noise down,
and they told me to get a life. 'I have a life'
I shouted back. 'I had a whole turkey to myself
on Christmas Day.'

HELP!

Last Christmas when I was very depressed
I rang the Samaritans and an automated
voice told me I was number 27 in the queue.

THE DIRTY MUG

You can get a refill of filter coffee
at Starbucks free if you bring your mug
back. I had no money that day, so gave them
a mug I'd picked up off a table, it had red
lipstick on it. They spotted my scam, but gave
me a coffee anyway. 'Nice lipstick you're wearing
sir' the assistant said.

THE DOCTOR'S OPINION

When I was in agony with sciatica,
I told my doctor if I'd had a gun
by my bedside I'd have blown my brains
out. 'No you wouldn't,' he said, 'I know you.'

THE SHORTER THE SAFER

I suppose if the average lifespan
was five hundred years, you'd eventually
get knocked down by a car in London and
probably get stabbed or shot at some point,
as well as getting bitten by some horrible dog
while out walking in the park one morning –
the shorter the safer.

SELF-HARM

He sold me his bike cheap –
said he wanted rid of it because
he kept wanting to put his foot
through the front wheel when he
was riding it – a little odd I thought.
And some years later when he was killed
rock climbing in North Wales I wondered
if it was deliberate?

THE DEAL

I once read in a newspaper
that a man was offered a
restaurant meal and all the beer
he could drink in an evening if he
killed someone. The man declined the offer
as I remember and grassed the guy to the cops.
You'd think he might have included a night in a hotel
and a good Havana cigar to round off the meal.

I'LL TAKE YOUR BLOOD PRESSURE

'Just relax' he said, 'try to relax –
relax for god's sake – it's going up.
It's over 160 – relax, relax damn it!
You're going to die if you don't relax –
it's nearly 200, you're not relaxing' and
that's when I fainted, the nurse told me later.

THE BLESSING

My friend took his cat
to a blessing of animals service
at his local church and it died
an hour later of a heart attack –
maybe it was an atheist.

FIRM HANDSHAKE

How I like shaking women's hands
after a night out with them –
it's so incredibly formal,
unsexist and unsexy – they just
don't expect it and you don't
get a visit from the Old Bill
ten years later on some sexual
harassment charge.

THE PEACE SHOP

Yes I remember the peace shop
in Glasgow, because I went there
once to buy a CND badge for a friend
and a fight broke out amongst the staff –
quite violent too, lots of things got smashed,
including a life-sized model of Gandhi. I, like
the other customers stood around perplexed, not knowing
whether to laugh at this unbelievable spectacle.
'Give violence a chance' somebody said afterwards.

SUITS ME

I was telling my friend's
ninety-six year old mother
about my twenty-one year old cat
and how I never expected him to live
so long when I got him as a six week
old kitten. She surprised me by being
quite dismissive. 'Oh you'll never get love
from one of them,' she said. 'They can't give
much affection.' 'Well neither can I' I said.
'That's why I got one.'

AGEING

I must look older than fifty-eight,
people are always offering me their seats
on trains and buses, holding doors open
for me, and my barber gives me the senior
citizens rate. I'm not complaining but time
has flown. It doesn't seem that long ago when
my mother only paid half-fare for me on the bus
into town and I was turned away from a cinema
because the film was an AA certificate, now suddenly
I'm an old man.

ASSISTED SUICIDE

I heard about someone who went
to the Dignitas clinic in Switzerland
with his family to end his life, but
after taking the lethal injection changed
his mind, jumped off the bed and started
running around the room shouting that he
didn't want to die, but it was too late.
He definitely didn't die with dignity.

ATTACK FROM BEHIND

London is so overcrowded these days.
As soon as you walk out of the house,
someone is following you. I always
stop and let them past and it's impossible
to scratch your arse when you need to.

THE MOANER

He was always complaining about his poverty −.
how he had no money to do anything,
but he was young and in good health and
I said to him 'There's always someone
worse off than yourself.' 'I don't think there is'
he said. 'Well I have a friend who is drinking himself
to death.' 'Well at least he can afford to' he replied.

RC

I always celebrate the massacre of
St Bartholomew's day – get drunk in town
with my friends from Opus Dei and look
for Protestants, heretics and other general
non-conformists to beat up.

1973

I was always a scruffy kid,
but this boy in my class said
I was smelly too – repeated it
several times. I suppose I should
have punched him, nipped it in the bud,
but I didn't and pretty soon the whole class
was calling me smelly. Some went even further
and called me a dirty smelly tramp, even a teacher
joined in. That was 1973.

YOU STARTED IT!

Knowing people as I do,
I'm surprised life isn't just
one continuous argument, as we
are really quite obnoxious creatures,
although we do our best to conceal it.
But I fear that the intrinsic horribleness
in us all will one day cause the argument
to end all arguments and wipe out the world –
you started it!

TEARS

How often have you been talking
to someone and noticed tears in
their eyes and think it's something
you've said that's made them sad or
they feel sorry for you in some way –
perhaps they know something you don't.
It can be a little unsettling, but I think
people's eyes just well up with tears sometimes –
like a cough can sometimes sound like a laugh.

CUTTING THE GRASS
FOR THE LESBIANS

His lesbian neighbours said it needed doing
and he volunteered immediately. It was a hot day
and he liked the idea of them seeing him with no
shirt on, despite knowing they weren't interested
in his body. He mowed the lawn for half an hour,
but to his disappointment they didn't look out
of the window once, even though he shouted for
a glass of water.

CHRISTMAS PRESENTS

My Jehovah's Witness friend said he was always
disappointed with his Christmas presents as a child,
one year he got a bag of elastic bands. His father
was an alcoholic and spent most of the money on booze,
and my friend told me he was quite glad when he fell
down the stairs late one Christmas Eve, broke his neck
and died. He had their rubbishy presents in a bag.

LAST RESORT

I met him running up Haverstock Hill
in his vest and underpants. 'What are
you doing?' I said. 'Can't stop now'
he said. 'I'm trying to get sectioned,
they've stopped my benefits.'

BLOOD

Surgeons see a lot of blood,
especially trauma surgeons,
they revel in the gory of it all,
but I wonder how they are in a fight –
I suspect they're mostly faint-hearted
wimps and I'd really like to beat one up,
or cut them with a sharp instrument and
watch them bleed, lose a lot of blood –
see the panic in their faces – no anaesthetic.

A JOB FOR LIFE?

He had been the Poet Laureate of Budgens
supermarket, Belsize Park – a post he held
for fifteen years, until he wrote a series
of strange poems attacking the Chinese,
which like all the others, he expected to be
displayed in the store, normally above the meat counter,
but the manager was having none of it. But it was only
when he was caught leaving the store with two bottles
of wine unpaid for, that he was finally dismissed from
the role.

HELL

I was talking to my friend Fr Michael
about hell and the eternal burning fire,
which doesn't destroy but preserves
what it burns. 'Oh no' he said, 'I don't
go along with all that. I think hell is
being stuck in a lift for eternity with
your worst enemy, suffering with severe
and permanent toothache, it makes more sense.'

IT'S BAD TO TALK

You can tell what people really think
about each other by the way they use
their phones – blocking calls, not ringing
you back, withholding numbers, having caller display –
permanent answerphone – speaks volumes.

A LIFE

What do people do with their long
dreary lives? How do they spend their time?
Sit in dark rooms breathing and listening
to their heartbeat, or maybe they sit on the toilet
for hours and think about dying. There is normally
time in a life to do most of the boring things on offer
and even repeat them should you choose – don't waste a
minute of it, you often hear it said, but you can't help
but really waste it all.

OVER IN A FLASH

London gets a lot of thunderstorms –
there was one today with lots of lightning
flashes. It's a cause of death I've never ever
contemplated, being struck by lightning, I've thought
about most of the others and I wondered if I would have moved
to London thirty-six years ago if I'd known I'd be struck
by lightning and killed here in 2019 – probably not.

DYING

They say that when some people die
the clocks in the house all stop,
birds of every kind appear at the windows
and cats and dogs howl. I hope none of these
things happen when I die, but I do get to see
my parents again fleetingly and the guy next door
hurts himself in his shed.

FEE

My friend from college days,
Mark Seaborn-Jones talked incessantly
about his father and what a great man he was –
a professor of psychology no less. He kept saying
I should meet him, but didn't invite me round to
his house. Then one day he told me that his father
was giving a talk at Liverpool University and I must come,
so I did and it was ten pounds on the door. He basically
charged me a tenner to meet his dad.

AT THE VET AGAIN

Well he's nearly twenty-two she said
and his kidneys aren't working that well
and he still has a heart murmur. You'll
probably have to think about having him
put to sleep soon. Would you be able to put me
to sleep too, I asked. I'm getting on a bit and
quite fed up actually – could you do us both together
at a special price? No, you'll have to go to Switzerland
for that she said.

ANARCHY IN THE UK

I used to walk on Hampstead Heath
every Monday morning with my Glaswegian
friend James. He had been in the army and
it was always a bit of a forced march,
but I enjoyed it. We used to stop for a smoke
in Dr Johnson's summer house, until it was burnt
down by Anarchists. I couldn't see what point
they were making.

REQUEST

Dear God let me die a neurotic's death –
an in my sleep death – not an ambulance
siren blazing rushed to hospital scary death.
Dear God let me die a coward's death – not a painful
operations, slipping in and out of a coma death.
Dear God let me die a timid death – not a bloody,
shocking violent death – let me die a spineless,
silent in my sleep death.

WRONG SEX

The Dominican priest had the sex-change
a bit late when he was forty. But after
being surgically transformed into a woman,
was asked to leave the order, as the Catholic
church doesn't allow women priests. His sister,
a nun who also had the operation was likewise
asked to leave the convent when she became a man.
I suppose they should have changed places.

BEING DEAD

She can't cope with the idea
of extinction – not existing.
I think she has a very strong
sense of self, more than most people,
almost narcissistic. It doesn't really
bother me though. It'll just mean returning
to the 1950's, a great decade for me – a doddle
in fact – no depression, anxiety or boredom –
just peace, I wasn't born.

WHY

What have I got on tomorrow,
dentist and launderette, yes,
I must give up smoking!

DEFIANT

I have a friend who is dying
of cancer and keeps booking
various trips abroad, which he then
has to cancel because he is too unwell
to go. It reminds me of when my mother
was in hospital dying – they used to send
a menu round each day and you would
tick the meals you wanted. Towards the end,
when she had virtually stopped eating, she would
still tick the boxes on the menu each morning.

GIRO DAY, 1981

I've got one egg left,
two rashers of bacon,
two slices of bread,
one tea bag, a drop
of milk and enough
toilet paper for one good shit,
but I get my giro tomorrow and
all will be well again.

TINKER FELL DOWN THE TOILET TODAY

My old cat fell down the toilet today
drinking from the bowl. I heard him
splashing around and helped him out.
I warned him it would happen, he's not
as agile as he used to be. I do give him
plenty of fresh water, but he seems to prefer
the toilet, which I think he regards as his own
private spring – there's no accounting for taste.

THE CROCK

I hated school and stayed off sick
quite a lot – faked it mostly, I was
just so unhappy there. The maths teacher
Mister O'Farrell shouted at me once.
'Off sick again Birtill. You'll toddle off
into an early grave.' And although I was only
twelve I liked the idea of dying and being dead
and was rather glad he'd said it.

LOSER

It must be very embarrassing
to start a war and then lose.
Hitler did and didn't just lose,
but was annihilated. No wonder
he shot himself, he couldn't live
with the shame and embarrassment –
couldn't face his friends, drink down
the pub anymore.

THE STUD

I remember once in Liverpool
seeing a beautiful blonde getting out
of a three-wheeler Robin Reliant and
then giving the disabled driver a long
lingering kiss. 'Is she your girlfriend?'
I asked him curiously. 'She's my wife'
he said. 'Likes fast cars then does she?'
'Don't be bloody stupid!' he said and limped
off down the road.

MEALTIMES

My cat has an overactive thyroid
and I have to give him a little
uncrushable white pill each day,
which I hide in his food. But quite often
he spots it and leaves it in the bowl,
so I have to try again. He must wonder
what it is. I think I would have been
rather alarmed, not to mention paranoid,
if one had kept turning up in the meals
my mother gave me as a child.

COFFEE MORNING

I knew he was a bit paranoid
and perhaps it was a mistake
to invite him round to my place
for a coffee one morning, but I
did anyway. 'And what's going in that?'
he enquired accusingly. 'Just coffee, and
milk if you have it' I said. 'And the rest!'
he shouted. 'Let's skip coffee' I said.

PAID FOR

I was drinking with him in the pub,
when he suddenly jumped up and said
there was something he needed to do –
couldn't put it off any longer. 'I've just
paid for my funeral' he said when he came back
smiling. 'Good to get it out of the way.'

THE OPTICIAN

I called his tests silly and unnecessary
and said they were taking too long.
He got his revenge by telling me I needed
to wear my glasses all the time, which I
later found out wasn't true.

REMEMBER MY NAME

I was telling my friend about a poet
I know who said his ambition in life
was to become as well known as possible
before he dies. 'Well I've never heard
of him,' my friend said.

SURPRISE

I remember one Christmas
when I was quite young,
my father gave me a piece
of asbestos neatly wrapped
in gift paper with a ribbon.
He said I could eat it.

FAME

Fame came late for Brendan Behan,
he had already been writing twenty years,
was a chronic alcoholic and it must have
seemed irrelevant. In my case success, not fame
also came late – in my late thirties and forties.
By then the party was over and I was overweight,
with grey hair. Fame should be enjoyed when you're young,
it doesn't really work in old age.

ODD

Once when I was at a party,
I was talking to this rather
boring social worker-looking type
with a beard and there was some
Ferrero Rocher chocolates on the table.
I took one and offered them to him.
'You know what the best thing is to do with these'
he said and crushed one into the carpet with his shoe –
a new carpet as well, it would have been difficult to
get out – I quickly circulated with other guests.

SOUR GRAPES

He's a failed novelist
and surprised me recently
when he said, 'It's a shame
so many women are writing these days –
it's more competition. A hundred years
ago hardly any did.' 'Well why don't you
go back even further' I said, 'to the time
when only monks could read and write – it would
have been even easier to get published.' 'Good point'
he said. 'I'm living in the wrong period.'

NO LONGER HERE

I was surprised to discover the comedian
Willie Rushton was dead recently – died
in 1996 aged 59. I always liked him and
used to think about him occasionally.
It's odd to think he hasn't been with us
all this time and me thinking he was still around.
I mentioned it to my sister who said she had the same
thing recently with Humphrey Bogart. 'But he's been dead
over 60 years' I said. 'Well I didn't know, did I.'

FRYING PAN

I bought it from Portobello market
and its colour was black, but a friend
who I had staying seemed to think it was
that colour because I hadn't cleaned it for years
and laughingly told people about it, until everyone
started calling me 'frying-pan' – I was known as frying-pan.
This didn't really bother me and I didn't even point out
his mistake. If people wanted to call me frying-pan it was
up to them – there are worse things to be called.

THE MAN WHO WALKS BACKWARDS

I didn't believe it at first,
until someone pointed him out to me –
the man who walks backwards in Camden Town.
Everything else about him seemed normal –
he was well-dressed and not agitated,
but he was walking backwards, quite naturally,
at quite a pace too. He'd been doing it for years
I was told, but nobody knew why – perhaps he preferred
looking at where he had been and not where he was going.

SPECIAL TREAT

My friend was telling me about
the time he went into hospital
to have his tonsils out.
He was only nine and put in a children's
ward. Shortly after the operation they wheeled
a big twenty-six inch screen television into the ward
and moved all the beds into a circle. My friend said
everyone thought they were going to watch a Western,
but it was Winston Churchill's funeral – it was supposed
to cheer them up.

I'VE STARTED SO I'LL FINISH

The guy just wouldn't shut up.
'I've started so I'll finish,
he would say. 'I've started
so I'll finish.' But no-one else
could get a word in. I ended up
telling him to 'fuck off!' I've
started so I'll finish' I said.
'Just fuck off!'

FINDING THE CHURCH

The first evening of our annual
summer holiday was always spent
looking for the local Catholic church,
unfortunately there was always one to be found,
which meant a long boring mass the next day.
But one year, I think we were in Abersoch,
North Wales, we couldn't find it. We walked
from one end of the town to the other, but no Catholic
church. What is this place! my father exclaimed –
bloody heathens, let them all rot in hell, but we had
an extra hour on the beach that Sunday.

HALLOWEEN

As usual a gang of annoying kids
started ringing my bell, so I opened
the window and told them to fuck off.
You can't say that, they shouted.
Yes I can, just fuck off! And don't
touch my car I said, pointing to my
neighbour's Jaguar. They all started
kicking it – he ran out shouting.

SPEECHES

My dad didn't think much of Oswald Mosley
when he saw him speak at the Manchester
Free Trade Hall in 1933. He went with a
socialist school friend who refused to stand
for the national anthem and was manhandled
by blackshirts. He was more impressed with Gandhi
whom he saw speak when he was living in India –
there was just something about him he said,
although he thought Mosley had better dress sense.
He was having two fillings at the dentist when he
heard Neville Chamberlain's 'We are now at war
with Germany' speech. It was an uncomfortable
feeling – all the drilling and the thought of being
called up.

SAMPLE

Just after he turned sixty,
his doctor's surgery sent him
a plastic bag and requested a
sample of his shit for bowel cancer
screening. He really enjoyed sending
them shit and the following week he sent
them some more and again the week after
and the week after that too. He even sent
them some dog shit from the street. He just
couldn't stop sending them shit, until he got
a visit from the police.

HOMESWAP

Some years ago when I was thinking
about moving out of London, I registered
with the council-run mutual exchange scheme.
Having a desirable spacious flat in Hampstead,
I got lots of offers, but was always changing
my mind and really messed a lot of people about,
including one couple in liverpool who even installed
a cat-flap in their front door for my cat. I often
wonder what their neighbours thought when this cat flap
appeared but no cat.

TREES

I was feeling a bit low
and talking rather negatively
about life. 'But just to live
for even one day and see the trees,'
she said. I knew she'd mention the bloody
trees, people always do. I'm sick of bloody trees,
I've seen enough of the things – what's
so special about them anyway. A lad I grew up with
fell from one once and was impaled on a branch which
pierced his heart and killed him – bloody trees!

DOZING

Catnap two in the afternoon,
wake suddenly with the very
intense thought that I will die soon
and go cold for a second. It doesn't
seem believable, not really, yet it's true
and the sudden realisation of it catches me
out again, as Larkin says – 'Most things may
never happen, this one will!'

JUST AN ACCIDENT

He spilt his coffee over my new carpet –
it was just an accident he said.
He knocked my dinner onto the floor in the pub –
it was just an accident he said.
He set fire to my sheets smoking in bed –
it was just an accident he said.
He dropped my mobile phone down the toilet –
it was just an accident he said.
He stood on my kitten and killed it –
it was just an accident he said.
He tripped me up and I fell through a glass door –
it was just an accident he said.
He managed to break my oven, washing machine,
fridge, toaster and lavatory seat – all accidents he said.
I pushed him in front of a tube at Leicester Square
and now he's in a wheelchair – it was just an accident,
I said.

OVERCOAT

He always wore a long coat,
even in summer, because he
liked having pockets he said.
But we all knew it was because
he had a big fat arse.

MORBID

No one really talked about death
and dying when we were kids, except
one lad, James Thompson, whose father
was the local funeral director.
He'd come out with odd phrases like –
'We'll all be dead in seventy years
and I'm going to be cremated when I die,
it's more cost-effective than a burial,'
and he was always saying 'You're a long
time dead.' Given that we were only ten
at the time, everyone thought he was a little strange

2020

I was talking to my rather mean friend
in Glasgow on New Year's day and asked
him how he saw in the new decade. 'I lit
a firework on the step at midnight' he said,
'then went back to my flat and had a tot of whisky
and some prunes.' 'Were you on your own?' I enquired.
'Yes, but I think my neighbour knocked, but I figured
she was after a tot of my whisky, so I didn't open the door.'

CAT

I got him as a beautiful six-week-old kitten,
but time came and went and eventually he died –
he was nearly twenty-two. I was as upset as when
my mother died, although there have been many intervening
human deaths since, none have bothered me too much really
and some I've been quite glad of. Human beings make a lot
of noise when they're alive and think they're very important,
but I don't miss them much, not like my cat – he was a far
better friend.

DREAMS

Dreams are a peculiar phenomenon –
dark, disturbing, occasionally uplifting,
usually a strange atmosphere. I think we know
they're not real, not really happening, but accept
the pretend world. It's like watching a film that
you are in – are the main character – extremely
entertaining, yet not serious – always different and
nearly alway in black and white, with so many extras and
exotic locations. Some unlikely people have a habit of
showing up too.

ENDGAME

My life's gone from bad to rubbish –
so many fine things have ended, are over –
finished and have not been replaced.
I really don't think I'll have many more
good days on planet earth now, so there's
only heaven to look forward to and contemplate
a better existence – it's a long shot I know,
but at least it's a bit of hope. They say no one's
ever come back, but why would they?

KILL ME

I got talking to her in the pub.
She'd just arrived in London and
needed somewhere to crash for the night,
so I invited her back. She was quite attractive,
but she didn't want sex; she wanted me to murder her.
'I know no one here,' she said – 'no friends or family,
no address – I'll not be missed if you kill me, but don't
use a knife.' I let her sleep in the spare room and
in the morning she seemed surprised I hadn't strangled
her in the night. 'You're not the murdering sort' she said.
'I'll have to try elsewhere.'

HITCHHIKING

He pulled up in this odd-looking contraption.
'Jump in' he said, but there was no seat,
so I sat on the floor. He said he only picked up
hitchhikers for stimulating conversation,
so I thought I'd better get talking, I tried football.
'You're boring me' he said. 'If you go on like that
you'll be out at the next service station.' Feeling
under pressure to be interesting I switched to politics,
but that didn't work either and sure enough I was out
at the next service station.

FINISHING

Sometimes when you've just completed
a long train journey, you imagine
how awful it would be to immediately
have to do it all over again. You may
have the same feeling after an exam –
a dental appointment or even a long walk.
I certainly had it leaving school after
five miserable years and I'm now beginning
to feel the same way about my life. I would
hate to have to go through it all again from
the start. I wouldn't give up my years for anyone –
I've earned them, it's been a hard slog.

GIVING UP

People are always giving up things -
alcohol, smoking, drugs, gambling,
chocolate, meat, caffeine, sugar,
salt, pornography. They acquire these habits
when they're young and spend the rest of their lives
trying to give them up – silly really. I don't intend
to give up anything myself, except life which I gave up
long ago.

VIRTUAL REALITY

He boasted over a thousand friends
on Facebook, but not one person
went to his funeral.

CORONAVIRUS

There's something rather eerie about it all -
like something out of a John Wyndham novel.
'It's all in the book of revelation' said
Father Michael – 'It'll be a plague of locusts next,
we're in the final chapter now – the day of judgement
draws near.' 'But you can't get toilet rolls' I said.
'Oh I wouldn't worry about that. I haven't wiped my
bottom in 25 years and I don't smell do I?'
'Well yes you do Father' I said.

EASING THE LOCKDOWN

My friend has been very careful
during the Coronavirus pandemic,
not wishing to be a daily statistic
as he put it. Even now when the death toll
is declining and they're beginning to lift
certain restrictions he's still not going out.
'I don't want to be remembered as the last person
in the country to die of Coronavirus' he said -
'just like the last soldier to be killed in the
First World War.'